THE SLEEPING DOGS OF LUBEC
BY RODGER MARTIN

The Sleeping Dogs of Lubec
by Rodger Martin

ISBN: 978-1-960293-17-6
First Edition
Library of Congress Control Number: 2025906747

Published by NatureCulture
NatureCulture Web Imprint
NatureCulture® LLC
www.nature-culture.net

Cover Design: Christopher Gendron
Cover Imagery: seals on a beach - Helgoland, Germany
by Vera Kuttelvaserova
licensed from Adobe Stock

Interior book design: Lis McLoughlin

The Sleeping Dogs of Lubec

BY

Rodger Martin

NatureCulture

Northfield, Massachusetts

The Sleeping Dogs of Lubec
Table of Contents

Mongrels

Acknowledgments

I am deeply grateful to poets Linda Warren and John Hodgen and scholar B. Eugene McCarthy for their insights and editing of manuscript and proofs. Not sure this horse would have ever gotten out of the barn without them.

DIRE WOLVES

Wolf

I own you well, wolf,
nuzzled in these dreams
and leafless stems of time.

In the three a.m. dark
my pad becomes your tread.
Your smooth, worn claws
glisten in the auroral light.

From Saginaw to Denali
your night wail echoes
off the canyon wall.

I watch, through your dark cornea,
the elk pick in the mist-choked swamp,

      and late at moon, wolf,

when the silence of my kind
erases the present, I taste
from your tongue
and feel the incisor cut
living from the dead.

Along the Monadnock Watch

I

Moonglow casts deep to the dark spine
and flank of this ancient whale of rock.
And here beached by the edge of a marsh
stream, like a salt, like an almost Roman
outpost, stands a well guarding hemlock
and brush while mist unveils its tapestry.

Soon a giant form thrashes clear of water;
a moose, rack erect, plods toward the well
and pauses. Steam rises from his back.
He slowly wheels, wattle winging like a bell
and sniffs toward the granite peak
that once sheltered wolf until these

near-sighted, almost Latin tillers ringed the stone
with flame and burned the green to ash.
The moose listens as those night legends sing,
then ignores the granite blocks and returns
to his slosh toward great lodges of pine.

II

Later, as the moon guards its lower track,
the moose is nailed on Highway 12, four limbs
shattered by the chrome of another dreamer.
An officer kneels by his side, strokes the dark fur.
The moose breathes deep; each slow release
a soft cloud masked in the flash of red and blue,
low crackle of voice, square box of rescue truck.

But there on the mountain framed under stars,
a gray wolf floats up the shoe-worn rock
and turns to stare down at the tiny strobes

gathered along the pencil line it cannot cross.
It sifts its head, then crouches low
and points its snout to heaven. The howl descends
to the ears of the valley. The moose awakens;
his clean, dark eyes meet the officer's. Natives awaken
and listen to owl echo wolf echo loon. The bull
imagines his antlers rising from a cold lake
while lilies cascade from his rack and he bellows.

The officer points his pistol and brings the hammer down.

Opera North

As evening darkens and the moon begins to thicken,
the slow, slender, rising howl of a wolf pours
onto the perfect pitch of November. Such want
shatters the illusion there's something in this earth
other than flesh and blood. Even an old man raking
his master's green must go wild under its spell.

It drives lost sailors to carve yard-long trenches
through the fog and ice of fire-rimmed beaches,
bleed them full and let shade after shadow slather
their lips with blood just to hear again the voices—
those shaped notes, the throat songs of their mothers,
the melodic high Cs that—if their ears remain
unplugged—might bear the vibrato of what is lost.

Or their boys who run from opera to hide in the rhythms
of a swing, watch grandfathers slowly roll their cigarettes.
But those voices snuff too, one by one, and the pendulum
of a swing set, the comfort of its arc, can no longer
scribe the physics to overwhelm that silence.

Boys, too, long for voices, find fellow soldiers, a tenor,
vibrant baritone, the harmony climbing beyond
the rifle pit lifting to the temple of a purple evening.
Even the enemy pauses, listens for one lost time.

Now old, old man, the wolf's lunar homage complete,
your raking done; find night. The wolf waits gently
your hand on its ruff. It pants easy in the blackness,
soft chorus, cool nuzzle, warm fur, faithful, faithful rest.

Cave of Chauvet-Pont D'Arc

An August storm darkens the afternoon.
I lean against the kitchen counter. My nails
split walnuts, pick the meat from shells,
and one after another slip them into the well

of my mouth—taste of time and its ancients:
Sunlight angles through the arc of a natural bridge,
brightens the brush, the white chalk of the gorge,
and reflects onto the blue murmur of the Ardéche.

Two mastodons cool and blow in the river.
Nearer, musky rhino muddy in a wallow.
Across, a pride of lions, belly-up and sated;
further, a herd of horses graze the meadow;

elsewhere the leopard sleeps on a limb until dusk.
The cave bear have gone far into the ridges, drawn
by the flourish of fattening berries. Birds flit then sing
to equilibrium's temporary lawn.

Here, beneath a laden walnut tree, the clan
congregates, focused by the fruit's fullness.
A couple grooms each other on the river sill;
children squeal beneath a dog patient as a saint.

Others husk, then split the shells, pop the lobes
one-by-one into their mouths, stretch, and yawn.
Holy, this moment, between was and will;
my fingers tremble with the urge to paint.

Memory of Hay Bluff, Brecon Beacons

Earlier, spring mist rolled itself into graying,
came down as drizzle; but now, it pours, clogs

buckets with rain, galoshes and sop, cats and dogs
roiling in the meadows, grass shin-high and praying,

pushing us back, daughter and I, to King Offa's dyke,
water swashing down our necks, trail a slither of slates

beneath sodden boots, drenched as two Centurions,
their maps soaked to paste, trudging into garrison.

Where had that breaching ramble brought us, ancient hike?
Two lording rings in search of answers; gussets, breastplates

rusting under endless slop leagues from Rome.
Too wet to talk. The Celts? Warm in their huts and home.

The trail funneled into woods. Mud and dusk fast
approached. Still the water came, and we slogged

with it downhill into the stone town at last
and a pub. Musk rose like steam. Rivulets eddied

beneath our feet. Warm fire, hot broth, mug of tea,
we drained among the book—wordless in this pluck

of fate—a bloodline baptized, dipped two thousand years.
We marvel still at our luck.

Webcam on the River Styx
—for Linda and Renate

Maritime dawn spots mirrored sunlight on a silent, moving river.
The black-and-white perpetual motion of an English Setter
flashes along the banks while I, the anonymous eye,
watch a woman in waders, carrying fly rod, mount an open boat
slowly poled by a She Charon across the Miramichi
to an Atlantic land and release of salmon. There,
on the bar, water washing stone of any deceit, they cast
the filaments of their lives in softly whistling "S's."
Again and again they place the ring of their offerings
perfectly before the eyes of their beholders.
Downstream, seven goslings in perfect line, paddle
behind their goose, the gander keeping them close
until they reach shore and choice grass then scatter
like children under the eyes of watchful parents.

Equestrian Sonnet for Him Whose Name Cannot Be Mentioned

High noon, our daughters ride proud;
their mares canter, strut, prance.
They know God herself dances
and snorts her way from mane to hoof.
Later my wife cuddles a buff kitten.
We argue names while the gnarly dog
thumps and sighs his way to bone.
I peer over the river marsh.
Equanimity, it could be Oxford,
farewell banquet on the Thames. My God,
for me you must be He who understands
the need to master, to sit and sip, to hear
the chants from Saint Martin in the Fields
distill five thousand years into a moment.

Foreclosure

Where in the cool evening breeze of the northern summer
does the bundled blanket lay for the heart to nest?
Like an abandoned kitten it mewls its hunger,
"Who will take me in? Who will take me in?"
But the unpainted clapboards frame an empty house.
The lonesome notes of the piano have long dissipated
and wild dogs rant in the driveway.
Oh round-eyed, down-covered kitty,
tail-shortened comet of the chest,
is a saucer of milk too much for this planet to give?

Sirius, The Dog Star

The Night Seals of Lubec

At witching hour, summer rain patters on the wharf;
fog drifts in and out to a tide just before change.
The seals glide to the landing, ease themselves from the water.
Respectful of whiskers, they nuzzle with their brothers,
the sleeping dogs of Lubec, reminding them of kinship.
Then, through the open windows of the town,
the seals silently enter the bedrooms of sleepers.
The dogs of Lubec curl contentedly on the floor
while the seals whisper in the ears of dreamers
who've mastered the seas at midnight
and charted the oceans of the past.
Then, silky as they had arrived, the seals
leave the sleepers for dawn, gather again
at the edge of harbor, nuzzle again with their brothers
and depart. When the children wake, they speak
of graceful dives through sun-greened kelp.
Their elders wake to puzzlement at a thin film of water
on the tiles that lead to open windows.

Scilly Boy

The tide has retired for the night.
The evening drifts toward darkness.
Beached boats splay on the draining sand.
Slack moorings, each tied to seawall-weathered rings
mark other plots as taken.
A boy and his young Setter pick along the tide line.
He unleashes the pup, brings out a ball
and arcs it along the sand.
The dog gambols to find it, mouths it,
prances, and finally galumphs it
back into the hand of the boy.
Again—and forth.
Bound—and back.
Sirius, brightest star in the heavens,
begins to twinkle. The galaxy winks in reply.
This way, then that.
Sky,
ball,
dog,
boy:
An elliptical ode to joy.

Bombogenesis

Like a whirlpool, like some swirling leak
draining a dammed river, eventually,
at some point, it all comes together:
That polar vortex screaming south,
snow crushed against the crunch of a boot;
a low clawing east like a hungry cougar
snatches the Gulf Stream by its throat.
Storm perfection, they waltz toward us and smile.
Winds fierce as wolves shriek out of the Northeast.
Waves pound dunes into submission.
Sand blasts skin off the cheek. Pellets
pile onto rooves until they collapse—another invasion.

Before this, other waltzes: The Anglos. Before
the Anglos waltzed the Norse. Before
the Norse, the Abenaki, before
the Abenaki, the Woodlands, before
the Woodlands, the Archaics and the Paleos.
Some left DNA, scattered like song
along the few rivers still flowing.
Others left juggernauts to ravage the landscape.

Blizzard after blizzard piles against our doorsteps,
this gate, bulging against the howl of ourselves. If it breaks. . .
the flood, the rot takes it all. No better, no worse
than those rhyolite points of the first invaders.
You—sustain this place like The Garden—or lose it.

Sequoia

The great arrows of honking geese echo low
over the marshes asleep within this northern range.
They migrate like Algonquin syllables, valley to valley,
lake after lake to the almost end of the Blue Ridge
and a Great Smokey evening where the dark shadow
of Sassafras stretches eastward like an enemy's cape.

He dreamt of characters, night long embraces, lines that threaded
codices, long walks that began at the cut of Genesee Canyon
and ended above cascades near Hawksbill. Later the clear dawn
streaked west, flashed like sun-bright tresses off the dome
of Mirror Mountain and foretold the white-haired man
with hickory canes who revised his tears, re-plotted the fall from grace.

Still, in spite of all that, for five hundred miles,
a peaceful man can meander The Parkway, coast the long,
horizontal fold of Tuscarora, sluice among the ancient
tongues which reverberate off the crests. He can wind
switchbacks and vertical slash of Black Mountain
until he reads the silence of great woolly cats
moving like padded verbs through the mist.
Here soft vowels whisper through gaps where bear
mark trees like impoverished souls; they scratch
the poles of virgin ash and leave their notes like prayer.

Love in the Time of Corona

—with respect to Gabriel García Márquez

Through the glass, in the cold March breeze, flaps
a neighbor's worn flag. Distance, like these bare branches—
white pine against blue sky—marks this corona,
this silver ring with dark heart. Loneliness is such I have
learned to look into the lens—that eye of defamation
in the hours before space made me miss the warm breath of another.
Somewhere a dog sighs on an empty bed. She has known all her days
this day would come. Sit with her. She is ready, willing,
will rest her head on your lap and speak with you in silence.

The Premiere

Noon against a brilliant August sun
the Colonial's marquee worked hard at glitter.

A stretch limo with vanity plate Tlitson waited curbside.
Its chauffeur stood at parade rest in navy cap and uniform.

Soon a small crowd: pastel gowns, black dresses, tuxes and tails,
crowded from inside. Two young women wore tiaras over coiffed hair.

Older women flourished scarlet or gold stoles about necks and shoulders.
One man strutted in his black Stetson. A photographer posed

first, each Tiara and then the Stetson on a director's chair facing the wall.
Each woman, shoulders poised above the star, smiled looking back

over the star painted on the back of the chair. The camera clicked again
as the Stetson took his turn, leaned back and propped a patent leather shoe

against a poster case on the theater's wall. Main Street traffic idled by.
Pedestrians in shorts paused to look, led their leashed dogs around the edges.

The three stars then piled into the limo and drove off. It turned right
at the corner, turned right at the next corner and as suddenly returned.

While flashbulbs flashed and a video cam rolled, the limo stopped
again in front of the theater. The formal crowd cheered and applauded

as the stars stepped out of the limo and walked back into the theater,
their make-up pasty under the sunshine, the pastels dull against the light.

Tone Poem Number Two

Beneath a sky duffed with fairy tales, in a field green as yesterday's rain, a horse folds her legs beneath and kneels herself into relaxation. She then invites a twelve-year-old girl to read against her flank. Soon two cats stretch out and join them. Finally their dog, old rogue that he is, swallows pride, lumbers over and flops beside them too. Such moments cannot last. You and I only think we know that.

They do not. How the cold knife of autumn slices into the flesh of tomatoes hung too long for table, turning their skin black with frostbite. Or the frozen hammer of winter fractures brittle tendrils of leaf into tiny flakes which waft into the sky and drift like humanity's ashes downwind to settle out of the dark smoke onto the snow. Or even the deep ooze of early spring taking all this and sucking it against one's boots, reaching up like jellied fingers, grasping for that last chance to deny before the lichen creep into the rock's mosaic and the green of this moment blossoms into now—the mare's sleepily drooping chin almost nudging the grass, the girl living between the lines of her story, the dog occasionally snapping at a fly, while the cats contemplate a hemisphere of silence.

Then, from a distance comes the rumble of sheet metal and combustion. Out of the noise, an olive-drab UPS van, dust smoking behind, barrels up the dirt road; a reminder life is hard-edged and relative. The dog remembers his rage, the girl her destiny, and the horse her fears. The cats? They startle then quickly regain their indifference.

All this was years ago. The dog is dead. The cats still practice religion, and the child has gone to woman. Occasionally, though, the horse will settle herself and lie in the middle of the field inviting someone to rest against her flank.

How does she know these rare chances for innocence? Know that reservoirs of peace are deep so need not be wide?

LET LOOSE THE DOGS OF WAR

The Merging Americas
  —*In response to a report about a Salvadoran surgeon's practice on junta prisoners.*

He was a fair boy. Did his delicate fingers
Aspire even then to become master surgeon's?
Did he dream doctors in perfect white
Drawing the scalpel to just
The correct epidermal depth—
While above, looking down, students watched
And, outside, a family prayed.

What denial opened his darker cells to the call
Of generals who promised respect and audience?
Was his family's bank account too common?
At least the State recognized skill,
Let him practice on enemies of the State.
When did his ego admire the local anesthesia so these patients
Could watch him exquisitely slice their abdomen,
Cut through their muscles,
Expose the cavity wherein men's guts could be tested?
                    With such gentleness he lifts
                    the rolls of white intestines out.
                    They so glisten in the harsh light.
Maybe the ingratitude of his patients' families
Or the failing health of The State sent him deeper,

That he later brought in his dogs—
Hungry like all dogs hunger
And let them feed on this rare sausage.

Our pets still love us,
Each wagging tail waiting its turn.
We so glisten in our own harsh light.

The Potomac

In our seasons of amorous bathing, Venus will loosen
her blouse; but during implacable years, it's Mars,
jock, who pulls tight the straps of his cod. So, chart
the offspring—a cupid or yeoman archer—the Potomac's
an arrow drawn across the bow of the Blue Ridge,
plucked at the drawstring of the Alleghenies.
Patriot always, the arrow aims at the heart.

Before this border became the great divide,
in the dry days, the dog days, when the river's
sweet waters swung low and like a murmuring
kiss brought the color-blind dark of night,
the river parted for the wheels of the underground
railway sending its children north to hide
among the rocky creeks of tributaries—

places with founders' names like Penn's Manor
of the Masque[1] where a boy, a ten-year-old's thrill,
could find bundles of food left at dawn
like manna, care packages wordlessly dropped
on his porch, and deliver them to stark faces
waiting beneath the dregs of McAllister's Mill,
Gettysburg, Pennsylvania, 1854[2].

---

[1] A land grant the Penn family reserved for itself from a treaty with the Indians of
land west of the Susquehanna River, part of which later became included York
and Adams Counties, Pennsylvania. Gettysburg became the county seat for Adams
County.
[2] See Bradley Schmehl's painting commissioned by preservationist Dean Shultz based
on an event contained in *Episodes of Gettysburg and the Underground Railroad* by J. Howard
Wert, edited by G. Craig Caba (Caba Antiques: Gettysburg) 1998.

Culp's Hill

John Wesley Culp, Gettysburg son gone down
to Winchester, enlisted, came home
invader. He visited first his sister,
then his cousin's farm—family stretched
taut as a tent trying to shelter all
from the thunderhead flattened to an anvil
that would hammer a quarter million
into submission: craniums split like melons,
the peculiar thwack and thud of bullet
hitting home. Home? What brought John Wesley?
The memory of toes wrinkling the water of Rock Creek?
The primeval odor of a breakfast cooked
while he slept?   Did he wake confused as the dog
from Steuart's Brigade leaping ahead of his master
as they charged the hill, determined to fetch
that imaginary ball bouncing in Union lines,
suddenly rocked backward.   Puzzled,
one leg shot away, the dog nuzzled gray bodies
for reassurance, a familiar scent.
And there, in the no-man's land between,
riddled from both sides, God's handy companion,
stretched for explanation, licked
a blue soldier's hand and died.
Later, General Kane ordered it buried,
the only Christian on the field.

And Wesley Culp, name pup-carved
into his rifle, played ball a few hours longer
by the fishing hole, in McAllister's Woods,
on McAllister's Hill, finally climbed a boulder
to catch a glimpse of Neill's lost brigade
and caught the ball in his forehead.
They left the family his rifle butt
folded like a flag.

Odysseus, Nemo, and the Warthog

Power, slap-happy W-K-N-E forecasts
Homeric fronts and soon black clouds roil down
the green ridges. Lightning splinters, hard
pellets of rain slash against the glass.

As a child I watched a slow twister spin
like Hermes and twirl up the long, tin roof
of a chicken coop. But this time, cool
Canadian winds push the dregs of Aeolus back.

Time to relax and enjoy the evening's re-blueing,
surround myself with family, Mozart, and dog.
Cuppa tea, legs crossed at the ankles
until the dervish whines of three A-10 Warthogs

barrel-roll east across the treetops.
Is it Christmas Eve that I leap to the sash,
barefoot across the deck, nostrils flared,
heart pounding like artillery and watch them

scalp out the roots of camouflaged tanks?
I squeeze my tongue and hold it all within.
Then, from behind, another low whine rockets up
the roof—an unexpected second flight

skits the shingles and as the shock splits
the crest, three more Warthogs boil
overhead. Hey-ZUES! I reach
for a weapon. The dog launches himself

and we shoot from our shells
like the Six Hundred in pursuit of six
A-10s training the weekend west.
Circe give him hawser and mast,

but the tale did not tell of later visits
while Penelope slept when Sirens jarred
twenty-five years and half-an-earth loose
in an instant. Must I always carry hemp?

War Dog Memorial
Barrington, New Hampshire

Next to the Veterans' Stone sits
an acrylic German Shepherd, panting
for command. In front, a small flag,
a whittled stick, and two large feathers
tied with leather which lift in the breeze.
Like an illusion, the evening summer
haze simmers about a drooping sun.
A distant lawn mower whines like a gnat.

Draped about the Shepherd's neck, dogtags:
Colonel, Roxy, Satan, Cochise. How easy
they trained—anxious, eager—man and dog,
while others strutted the suited wire of duty
and looked down, knowing the dogs
would sense too late, in that sudden crash
of automatic weapons, recognize
like their men all had been forsaken.

The wind turned on my cheek. I saw
Old Barley lift himself at each
late-night mission, wait by the door
acknowledgment and after plod to his bed,
circle three times, and drop, one great sigh
escaping as he drifted into sleep.

Prayer, Christmas Eve, for Recovery of My Dog

O Magnum Mysterium shoulder me lightly
like a clear river carries an autumn leaf
away on a current of harmony, beyond
this concrete bridge where breath and brain
track the secrets in this dog's flesh
panting here before me with his three legs
and thumping tail. Too soon his lungs will fail.

Or over there, just beyond the road,
the memory of my brother's child
crushed between the wheel and the hood,
the accordian of her auto pressed to the bark, *Oh
Tannebaum*, before gasoline lit
that perfect conifer in one great choir,
searing ornament to a father's Joyful Season.

Or further down that road a mother, things
that made her cut—a vain attempt to purify
for Holiday, and so she comes to pass one evening
a bag of bones and tumor lying in a bed,
and all a boy can do is drum this nativity away.
Pray? That she could run, like the dog in his dreams?
What can children do for their mother but live?

Or beneath the midnight star—raw earth silent
after the battle's pageant—a shrapnel-clad soldier
lying in a crater, medic kneeling over him,
hands pressed against the sucking chest wound,
eyes searching for the angel of any medivac
to appear in the dark above and tally them both
to manger before the Magi's gifts give out.

Only wander does wonder to relieve this beauty,
this annual thrust to blackness. Gracious God
reaching from beyond the nebula, cradle me,
small wren stunned by the window, through this birth,
so I may again walk with dog the village green and pause
where for eight-hundred years grandfathers paused
to contemplate solstice and in that softening evening hear

acapella voices sing *In Dulci Jubilati*
and recover the faith of my father, my dog, and my God.
"... Oh that we were there. Oh that we were there."

PUPPY LOVE

Aztec Fable

Autumn's the strange time. The sky is ancient blue. A flick of sun angles like a dream over a leaf-stirred pond where a bone-aged poet creeps and crawls, calling to his apprentice, "A good time to be lonely, to seize that lucid last look before cold clamps…" He stops.

"The digits and gangrene blackens the spring-fed eye?" his apprentice responds.

With the dawn of every lesser day the teacher pushed this dead news gently, "Look, the oak wave their caution, the maples bark out stop. They cannot hide their gold."

"Sure," counters the boy, "like eagle corporate papa dogs, director feathered, board-room majestic. They preen in three-piece greed. Their talons reach even here, turning to snakes, squeezing hearts through the mouths of billions. Magic brokers, mighty achievers—like your Aztec, your Toltec—they strut before the altar of the bill and lift toward this same sun handfuls of dripping, beating wealth. They bleed themselves horny while rock-frenzied crowds suck up the fraud then mosh out the dregs at the foot of the temple."

"Yes," the old man sighs, even my Aztec, and for you too there will come a day of choice, a sole great hour of sharing like the phone's insistent ringing, or the traffic's constant hum or the screen's incessant drone—a trinity of options, the saviors of your time—just like those of mine. And you must reach for your potter's mug braced with steaming chocolate, palms cupped about its heat, bring it to your lips, sip, savor, press the mug against your cheek—"

The younger interrupts, "You mean ignore *The New Yorker's* voice? The put down? And wait for a time of eclipse? No! I'd rather stomp like Cortes in the blue, thin-aired dawn, crest a volcanic ridge, see spread beneath and before afloat on a lake like a bridal cake, my metropolis glistening, its causeways spidering out empire and god. Montezuma, supported on the arms of his lords promising gold, promising silver …. And like Cortes swollen inside his armor say, 'I, Smoking Mirror,

Quetzalcoatl, strangler of wives, come from the East to fill this valley with fumes.'"

"You could," the old man carefully chooses, "or you could note the woman between—her redwood dugout plying the waters of words which separate gods and facts and faith. See the child that hummed at her nipple. She knew nothing but children could be saved so wove them into feathers and songs which wrap us still, turn us from the glass and steel bullets which ricochet off these elevated boxes, these mausoleums, our vaults sheltering our brokered genteel. I chose my Malinche, her body the dark side of the moon, a mystery that drags me daily here to you, my survivor. You, who must—some chill and hung-over morning—reel from the conquest of a Manhattan where Cortes swaggers above the skyline, his helmet gleaming in the ozone; his breastplate mirroring the sun, leather breeches taut above the skyscrapers, one boot planted atop each Twin Tower and his mailed fist pushing forward a gold-encrusted cross.

"With his other glove, he reaches for Montezuma, tottering atop the lightning rod of his empire like a Kong swatting flies. They will both tumble down this scrape of conquest. Only pastel of words, a woman and her ruby throats—iridescent in their nectar, the reds, the greens— the language of a garden. These dart backward, frontward, naked as the morning and the glory. Cradle the plush pile of her growing long, circle her flame, suckle her milk and ring our bursting bells of story."

"How? How will I know?" asks the younger.

The elder raises his aging frame, "How? The more you know, the less. Then you'll choose to bundle up for spring. Autumn is the 'know' place. It keeps us balanced enough to grow."

A Poet Must Brunch Alone

Alone, the frittata's sauce touches the need
to believe. Taste deep as tongue spreads
down the spine's pores and hungers
like an aborigine, crouched before red
sandstone hungers, the sound
of his digiri bounding, winding
across the scrub. He sniffs,
fresh from the outback's oven,
his olfactory rising like bread.

Alone, a dark glass of Montepulciano
worships mystery beneath a vineyard moon.
Like a wolf's yowl echoes across an escarpment,
it yearns for the ears of its partner
trotting the edge where she pauses
to let the warm breeze rise
and rustle the ruff of her neck.

Alone, an orange cuts freshness into rosettes
like a jaguar silently padding a river's bank.
Its yellow eyes scrutinize the least uncertainty
ready to spring, to lock jaws
'round a cranium of doubt and with one
omniscient bite, convert the mind's shell first
into lunch, then into life, and last into thought.

Beyond the Edge of Beethoven's *Ninth*

The concert master rises, lifts a violin,
and draws a bow across its strings.
His wife tunes her cello to him
and waits. Their daughter, front row, slumps—
an adolescent slink—which tries to disguise the sparkle
hidden, like a full, coronal eclipse, behind her eyes.

Twelve years ago, her father taught my child
to grasp a violin's neck and hold her wrist level,
supple. Then, interrupting Haydn's pity,
Schubert's ache, the studio door swung open,
his wife, haggard, baby screaming at her breast,
dark bags beneath eyes too tired to care
simply stood in silence. . . .

Somehow, some way, those three are here now,
a dialectic of brilliant instruments, apex solid
as Cheops, like that deaf composer's search
of memory who found in the choral fantasy
of his youth chords triangulated to save him,
the call and response of leader and pack
like two great Newfoundland puppies at play
gamboling under the eye of their mother
forward in time, to give in this moment,
in this place, to this blind man—
sight, to this mute man—voice.

Collie Writer

Fresh in from the whirlwind
of her stroll, she leaps onto the sheets
and rolls and rubs, and then—poem complete—
retires to the carpet, leaving well-spaced
a pine needle, three small green burrs,
and some dew from the lower lilac.
She curls herself and raises one eyebrow, "Well?
What do you think?" I ponder my critique,
"It's good," I say. "Great parallel structure,
and the three burrs make superb layering of possibilities.
But—that mud-print on the pillow—not sure the poem wants
to go in that direction." She raises her nose, sniffs and looks away
as if to reply, "What do you know about poetry."

Ode to Spot the Tongue
—after a visit to the dentist

Oh great Laplander of organs,
metaphoric Labrador's nose in homo sapiens,
inconsolably curious, irrepressible
in its tactile snuffing about the hydrants
of the mouth, searching to discover that odd
flavor and—tasty fragrance discovered—
uncontrite in its revisiting,
panting, lolling, licking the scent
until attentiveness at last erodes
the oddity to a familiar cusp.
Spot the Tongue cannot be trained
though it will sit and bark and beg,
then roll over to the vacuity between the ears
of those imagining themselves smartest
in the office. How the tongue fools us
with words until the next piece of cutlery
tautens the Etch-a-Sketch bib
draping the animal of ourselves
and deletes everything we trained it
to know.

Ms Cat

Oh great puzzle, sphinx of fur, Isis of calm
observing the two great Newfoundland puppies
like Grendel's children at play gamboling toward you—
eye of the universe, focus of light.
Educator of the unwise, sentinel of manners,
you slowly stretch your paws
and patiently extract your claws.

Mongrels

Policing North Road at Eighteen

His Long Trail now Two Roads diverged in
yellow woods, the Red Bull with Banded Horn,
devoid of energy, rests with that little nip, Jack Daniel's,
inside the pasture fence. And she of Newport, an empty package,
puffs next to a Busch, listless as Narragansett at low tide.
But what does Genessee on the other side? A craft
to Harpoon Sam Adams? A Rolling Rock?
Regardless whether Heiniken or can't,
Smuttynose even a St. Pauli Girl, would not drink
White Claw sparkling water from a can
which makes Budweiser then Bud Lite.

Translation of a Poem by My Dog Barley titled "Truck Drivin' Dog"
—with respect to X.J. Kennedy plus any appropriate truck driving music

Oh, I'm a truck driving dog.
So there ain't nothing in this world
that I love better than to jaw
a shiny bumper pick-up right off of my road!

Howling at the moon,
arfing at the rubber,
running with the lubber
who thinks he's got me covered,

I'm a truck driving dog.

Give me all seasons on a Monday,
pneumatic on a Tuesday, then some wide tread,
some 4-ply and by Friday
I'll chomp the best steel radials in the whole damn world

'cause I'm a truck driving dog.
So there ain't nothing in this world
that I love better than to jaw
a shiny bumper pick-up right off of my road!

And on weekends I hang about the shed
till the boss picks up for the dump
where my Bessie growls at all the hounds
so I get the blues while I sit on my rump.

Oh, daddy, get me to the dump on time.

And then I sniff her once or twice
while the boss recycles his trash
and before he's gotten his garbage away
we've had our quick flea-bitten bash.

I'm a truck driving dog.

She's a loose-jowled shaggy bitch
still I love her just the same
because she's never had the rabies
and her arthritis has got her lame.

      I'm a truck driving dog.
      So there ain't nothing in this world
      that I love better than to jaw
      a shiny bumper pick-up right off of my road!

And if I'm elected to the board at Beebok
I'll tell you what I'm going to do:
I'll order a line of rotten sneakers
and give all the yuppie puppies a chew.

      Yes, I'm a truck driving dog.

You see my life is dedicated
to the things I itch to do
so if you cool cats don't like it
than it's ruff-tough canine shit to you

      Oh, I'm a truck driving dog.
      There ain't nothing in this world
      I love better than to jaw
      Pick-up trucks, Beebok pumps, flea-bit hounds, fuzzy cats

So stay off of my dirt, GRRRRRRRR.

High Noon at The Covid Corral

Ro and I go way back, back to the days when she was Rory, a ninety-pound American bulldog putting out litters behind the newspaper's office, and I was putting out fires from people who never asked themselves the question, "What could possibly go wrong?" The first time I saw her—well, her name began with R-o and my name began with R-o. It was love at first spelling. She could out-eat and out-drink any word-slinger we ever met. Today everyone knows us as Ro-Ro.

One day we said to hell with litters and fires and took off for the freedom of the Wapack Trail. At night we'd sit on the edge of a mountain meadow, campfire blazing, looking over the twinkling lights of the little towns below and I'd pluck my bouzouki, sing a mournful tune. Ro, she'd join in, and soon we'd have the heavens trembling.

In the morning, I'd buckle up my journalism belt loaded with a reporter's six-pack in each holster. Ro she'd strap on her six guns, hung low and slow over her hips. Why her pistols jingle-jangled against her dew claws as she John Wayned herself beside me along the trails into town.

Over the years, life on the road got real cold in winter, so we decided I'd take up teaching at a college and Ro, she'd take up napping at home. It worked out well for awhile.

Then came Covid.

And every week I had to get tested. Ro was fine with that, of course, because she'd come to enjoy sleeping late while I got tested. Each week I got a different colored wristband with a new number and so long as it claimed I was clean, I could come to work (sporting a mask of course). Every week I tested and every week I got a clean bill.

Other then the mean-hombre look of the mask, it was a good life because I got to train students how to put out fires and then write stories about those who didn't ask the question, "What could possibly go wrong?"

One afternoon came an e-mail telling me I didn't get tested. I huffed and puffed and told them I had been tested. Ro woke from her nap, eyed me casually, rolled over, and went back to sleep. But then came a second e-mail stating I was banned from campus until I got a clean bill of health. It's one thing to be officious and right. It's another thing to be officious and wrong. As I said before, "What could possibly . . .?"

The huffing had evolved into the Ro-Ro Gang language that used to get edited out of a story. Ro (That's her.) woke up and said, "Ro, (That's me.) what's all this cursin' about?" Ro (That's me.) said to Ro (That's her.), "Look at these e-mails." Ro (That's her.) read them, bristled, roused herself on all fours, and said, "Ro (That's me.), No one messes with my man. You are going in to town now, right to that testing place, and I'm going with you."

Ro and I hopped into our 1980 Ford F-250 rust bucket and bounced onto the road. It was as if we were out on the trail again, and we were loaded for bear.

We roared into the gymnasium parking lot, stepped out and slammed both doors. Things had gotten real quiet. Campus safety officers took one look at the two of us and began ushering young people and faculty back into their classrooms. Appian Way was deserted as the two us sauntered John Wayne style, my journalism notebook in my holster and Ro giving the evil eye to every hombre who wanted a piece of her man.

The long lines at the gym sign-in stations disappeared as if it was the Clanton Gang rather than the Earp Brothers riding into Keene. Inside, I had my choice of a dozen empty sign-in seats with a dozen shaking clerks. We chose Number Six.

The woman behind the table shivered and stammered trying to explain someone had mistyped my address on the keyboard and that I had two ID numbers, not one. Ro (That's her.) growled, "Step aside" and the woman quickly stepped aside and ran off. Ro plumped herself into that vacant seat, then proceeded to sit on that keyboard until it squealed, and then raised herself and faced everyone in the gymnasium down saying, "Any Objections?"

Silence.

Finally a group of EMTs rushed to our side pleading, "May we please help you to the testing station," where another EMT trembled so much he couldn't get the nasal swab from its package.

Ro again growled, "Step aside."

The trembling EMT dropped the swab packet and stepped aside. Ro (That's her.) put one paw on the package to hold it down and with her teeth, ripped the paper off, then offered the swab to Ro (That's me.) But before I could take it, she shook her head no, stuck the swab into her mouth, rolled it for five seconds, then spit it into the glass vial with my name on it. She scanned the gymnasium carefully, "Any questions?"

Silence.

Ro (That's her.) gently picked up the glass vial just as she'd picked up her litters of pups and carried the vial over to the sign-out table where she expertly dropped it into its proper place in the carrier. Then she whipped herself around, eyed every being in the gym, "Now, is my man going to get his test results on time? Or do I have to pay a second visit?" She followed that with a low growl that vibrated the rafters.

Every Jack-a-muffin in that space nodded, stuttered and smiled weakly. The Number Six clerk who had run off said, "No, no, I mean yes, yes, he'll be fine. We just love him to come and get tested. Tests will be in his folder in 24 hours. Good doggie, please, may we pet you?"

Ro snapped her jaws and rolled her head around her massive neck then harrumphed, "Good." Finally she leapt straight into the air, wheeled 180-degrees to land, tail high, facing the exit. Ro ruffled her fur, she looked back at Ro (That's me), nodded toward the door and said, "Let's go."

As the evening sun settled over the Ashuelot River, Ro-Ro sauntered slowly, Marion Morrison style, out the back side of the gymnasium, their holsters jangling, one set against his jeans, the other against her dew claws.

Variation on a Theme

Ein gutes haustier ist ein hund.
Er bëlt so laut; er ist gesund

Great dog, lap stashed and easy, lay on the passenger seat,
exhalations deep and content from the galumphing,
noggin propped against the dash.   Speak to me tongue.
Lick satisfaction on this present mobility of pleasure.

Roll me again your smiling sigh and stomachy growl
that I may know, here in the vehicular center
of the universe, one being knows all one needs—
despite the absence of consonant and vowel.

The Last Supper

When a guest told his dinner mates,
"I'm going to move my horse,"
they thought figuratively, like good poets.
When, in ten minutes, he didn't return
they sent, metaphorically speaking, the host
to check the john. The host found no worse
than *Explanation kind* so they
created the form this lyric must take
when suddenly the guest appeared again,
his horse stabled safely, watered and grained.

Language is the *Cannon Ball Express* puffing across
its trestle of letters balanced barely above the gorge
so that if the chugging stops, the bridge will collapse
and the leap becomes literal, not some Bunji jump
that can be taken back.   The guest can only hope
the river runs full with clear, spring melt.

And if he survives the struggle to shore,
he will hear contrapuntal harmony
and will follow the voices wherever,
even into the relic of a church,
to stand transfixed when the singing stops
and its echoes strike him numb
like a dog freshly runover,
wobbling in wonder,
quizzical to the end.

Molly

As sea waves of grief wash over the sand, know
this a necessary acknowledgment of loss.
Know, each recession of cleansing, salty liquid
erodes a grain or two of pain. Know her spirit
footloose and free of limit, again splashes
along the beachy shore of an ocean. Know
she gifts these tears, these memories:
preparations for the heart to blossom again. Know.

Quantum Thinking on a Painting and Juli Nunlist's poem "Viewpoint"

If I, like the poet and a painter mending a fisherman's net,
am looking one way at filaments of mesh,
or another way at bounded holes, I am
like Schrödinger's cat, both shadow and substance.

So, let the two of us tango through the October sunlight
toward the brook and the trail, a portal to pine woods
slowly transforming to winter. Within this cat, at this instant,
just as ferns creep over the yellowed path, a particle,
shadow and substance, *enchuflas* left, and somewhere across
the sliced breadloaf of universes, countless parsecs apart,
perhaps even at the crust of one loaf, this particle's twin
and its shadow also dances identically left, simultaneous,
in both time and space, both filaments of net and bounded holes.
And if I have one quantum twin, why not ten, or thousands, or trillions?
Each creating me and my *homoousious* me, content, smiling,
and moonwalking across the bread and star shine of both.

Acknowledgements of Previous Publication

"Wolf," *Appalachia*, Winter 1984-1985, Vol. XLV, No. 2, Appalachian Mtn. Club, Boston, MA; republished in *The Nemo Poems: A Martian Perspective*, Northfield, MA: NatureCulture, 2025.

"Along the Monadnock Watch," *Monadnock: More than a Mountain*, www.monadnockmountain.com, *Heartbeat of New England*, 2007; *Heartbeat of New England: An Anthology of Contemporary Nature Poetry*, James Fowler, Ed., Tiger Moon; *Contemporary Foreign Literature*, No. 31998; *Lungfish Review*, Vol. 1, No. 1, 1993, *The People's Voice*, Vol. 1, No. 18, August 25, 1993.

"Tone Poem Number 2," *The Occasional Moose*, Peterborough, NH: *The Monadnock Ledger*, November, 2004.

"War Dog Memorial," *The Black River: Death Poems*, Northfield, MA: NatureCulture, 2024. *The 2008 Poets' Guide to NH*, Poetry Society of New Hampshire, 2007, p.11.

"Molly," *The Black River: Death Poems*, Northfield, MA: NatureCulture, 2024.

"Webcam on the River Styx," *Miramichi Reader*, Jan. 23, 2024, *Smoky Quartz: Tenth Anniversary Anthology*, Monadnock Writers Group, 2022.

"Collie Writer," *Poets Touchstone*, Vol 65.1, Spring 2023.

"The Night Seals of Lubec," *Migrations and Home: The Elements of Place*, Northfield, MA: NatureCulture, 2023; *Crosswinds*, Vol. IV, 2019.

"Bombogenesis," *Writing the Land: Maine*, Northfield, MA: NatureCulture, 2022.

"The Cave of Chauvet Pont d'Arc," *PoetrySky 58*, Poetry Quarterly (poetrysky.com); Spring, 2021; *The Worcester Review*, Vol. 33, 2012.

"Policing North Road at Eighteen," *On and Off the Road: Poems of New Hampshire*, ed. William Chatfield, Peterborough, NH: Peterborough Poetry Project, 2020.

"Scilly Boy," *The Scillonian*, No. 288, Winter, 2018.

"Prayer, Christmas Eve, for the Recovery of My Dog," *Imago Dei: Poems from Christianity and Literature*, Abilene Christian University Press, 2012; *Christianity and Literature*, Vol. 52, No. 4, Summer 2003, State University of West Georgia.

"Memory of Hay Bluff," *Shadow and Light—A Literary Anthology on Memory*, Peterborough, NH: Monadnock Writers' Group, 2011.

"The Last Supper," *Diner: A Journal of Poetry*, Poetry Oasis, Spring/Summer, 2001.

"Equestrian Sonnet for Him Whose Name Cannot Be Mentioned," *New Hampshire College Journal*, Vol. XVIII, Spring, 2001.

"Sequoia," *Sahara: A Journal of New England Poetry*, Vol 1, #2, Fall/Winter 2001. Worcester, MA: Elizabethan Press.

"Odysseus and the Warthog," *Ad Hoc Monadnock*, Peterborough, NH: Monadnock Writers' Group, 1995.

"Opera North," *The Blue Moon Series*, Concord, NH: Hobblebush Books, 2007.

"The Potomac," *The Battlefield Guide*, Concord, NH: Hobblebush Books, 2010.

"Culp's Hill," *The Battlefield Guide*, Concord, NH: Hobblebush Books, 2010.

About the Author

Rodger Martin's *For All The Tea in Zhōngguó* (2019) follows *The Battlefield Guide*, (Hobblebush Books: 2010, 2013) and the selection of *The* Blue Moon *Series*, (Hobblebush Books: 2007) by *Small Press Review* which was one of its bi-monthly picks of the year. Most recently he has been a major contributor for NatureCulure®'s *Writing The Land*® anthologies.

Martin's distinctions include serving as a New Hampshire State Council on the Arts in Education roster artist and a touring artist for the New England States Touring Foundation, administered by the New England Foundation for the Arts. He has done artist-in-residency programs throughout New England. In 2012, he represented the United States as one of twelve poets participating in the City of Hangzhou's literary festival on West Lake, China. In 2015 he was a visiting poet at Nanjing University and Shanghai University of International Business and Economics, where in 2017 his poem "The Anchor" has been mounted at the reflecting pool where it was inspired. He returned to Yancheng with six other American poets as part of the *Poetry Bridging Continents III* Conference.

His awards include the 2024 Stanley Kunitz Medal for his lifelong commitment to poetry; an *Appalachia* award for poetry; a New Hampshire State Council on the Arts award for fiction; and fellowships from The National Endowment for the Humanities to study T.S. Eliot and Thomas Hardy at Oxford University and John Milton at Duquesne University.

In 2018, Meg Kearney chose one of Martin's poems for permanent trail mounting at Cathedral of The Pines. His publications include literary journals and anthologies throughout the United States and China where he also wrote a series of essays on American poetry for *The Yangtze River Journal*. He and six colleagues, as part of The Monadnock Pastoral Poets, have been featured in a new book *On the Monadnock: New Pastoral Poetry released in China in 2007.* 2013 marked the completion of a decade-long project with Dr. B. Eugene McCarthy to adapt all twelve books of the epic poem *Paradise Lost* for dramatic reading. His critical work "The Colonization of Paradise: Milton's Pandemonium and Montezuma's Tenochtitlan" published in *Comparative Literature Studies* broke new ground in Milton studies.

In addition to his writing, Martin teaches journalism and Creative Writing at Keene State College, co-advises *The Equinox*, the college's award-winning student news organization. He was managing editor of *The Worcester Review* for almost three decades, and for six years he directed New Hampshire's Poetry Foundation's Poetry Out Loud Project.

Rodger Martin was born in the amish country of Pennsylvania, lived in England as a child, and served as a combat engineer in Vietnam.

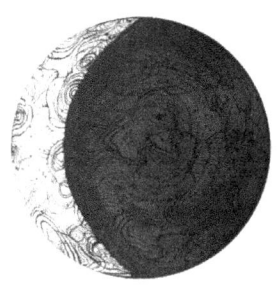

About NatureCulture Web

The mission of NatureCulture® is to help humans be in right relationship with the rest of the natural world. NatureCulture Web is our new imprint for books brought to us by like-minded authors and organizations.

Please see all NatureCulture's publications at:
https://www.nature-culture.net

Other NatureCulture® Books

2025
Dark Matter: Women Witnessing, Dreams Before Extinction, eds. Weil, et al
The Nemo Poems: A Martian Perspective, by Rodger Martin

2024
The Black River: Death Poems
ed. Deirdre Pulgram-Arthen
Cayman Brac From Bluff to Sea
Writing the Land: The Connecticut River
Writing the Land: Wanderings I
Writing the Land: Wanderings II
Writing the Land: Virginia
Wriring the Land: Maine II, A Gathering

2023
Writing the Land: Youth Write the Land
Writing the Land: Currents
Writing the Land: Channels
Writing the Land: Streamlines
Migrations and Home: The Elements of Place, ed. Simon Wilson

From Root to Seed: Black, Brown, and Indigenous Poets Write the Northeast, ed. Samaa Abdurraqib

2022
Writing the Land: Foodways and Social Justice
Writing the Land: Windblown I
Writing the Land: Windblown II
Writing the Land: Maine
LandTrust, poems by Katherine Hagopian Berry

2021, 2024
Writing the Land: Northeast

Forthcoming (2025-2026)
Writing the Land: The Rensselaer Plateau
Writing the Land: Washington
Writing the Land: Doolin, Ireland
Writing the Land: The Cayman Islands
Writing the Land: Pathways
Writing the Land: The Great Forest of Aughty

www.ingramcontent.com/pod-product-compliance
Lightning Source LLC
Chambersburg PA
CBHW051242120626
46547CB00014B/1764